T

from

Lewis W. Hine **CHILDREN AT WORK**

Lewis W. Hine
CHILDREN AT WORK

By
Vicki Goldberg

Prestel

Munich · London · New York

Lewis W. Hine: Children at Work

Front cover: Breaker boys, Ewen Breakers, South Pittston, PA, 1911 (page 72)
Page 1: Minnie Thomas with her sardine knife, Eastport, ME, 1911 (page 100)
Frontispiece: Howard Lee, Wheaton Glass Works, Millville, NJ, 1909 (page 85)
Spine: Shrimp picker, Biloxi, MS, 1911 (page 94)
Back cover: Addie Laird, spinner in a cotton mill, North Pownal, VT, 1910 (page 53)

Library of Congress Catalog Card Number: 99-62961

© Prestel Verlag, Munich · London · New York, 1999
All photographs by Lewis W. Hine courtesy of the
National Archives Still Picture Branch, College Park, Maryland
Photographs by Jacob A. Riis and Jesse Tarbox Beals in the
introduction courtesy of The Museum of the City of New York,
Jacob A. Riis Collection
Portrait of Lewis Hine in the appendix courtesy of the
George Eastman House, Rochester, New York

Prestel Verlag
Mandlstrasse 26, D-80802 Munich, Germany
Tel. +49 (89) 38 17 09-0, Fax +49 (89) 38 17 09-35
4 Bloomsbury Place, WC1A 2QA London, England
Tel. +44 (171) 323-5004, Fax +44 (171) 636-8004
and 16 West 22nd Street, New York, NY 10010, USA
Tel. (212) 627-8199, Fax (212) 627-9866

Prestel books are available worldwide.
Please contact your nearest bookseller or write to any
of the above addresses for information concerning
your local distributor.

Edited by Peter Meredith
Designed by Maja Thorn
Typesetting and Lithography by LVD, Berlin
Paper is Galerie Silk 200 g/m^2 (Schneidersöhne)
Printed and bound by Sellier, Freising

Printed in Germany on acid-free paper

ISBN 3-7913-2156-0

Contents

LEWIS W. HINE, CHILD LABOR, AND THE CAMERA

Vicki Goldberg

In this boasted land of freedom there are bonded baby slaves,
And the busy world goes by and does not heed.
They are driven to the mill, just to glut and overfill
Bursting coffers and the mighty monarch, Greed.
When they perish we are told it is God's will,
Oh, the roaring of the mill, of the mill!
—ELLA WHEELER WILCOX

The history of photography is not a single strand but a braid of intersecting histories, prominent among them a history of technology, a history of vision, and a history of culture and cultural attitudes. Thus rapid motion could not be photographed until emulsions and lenses had reached a level responsive to Eadweard Muybridge's ingenuity, an audience for the modernist photography of Paul Strand's "Picket Fence" probably did not exist before cubist painting created one, and Lewis Hine's social documentary photography of child laborers would not have occurred before American ideas about poverty shifted.

The traditional view of poverty was that in a land of democratic opportunity people were responsible for their own conditions; the poor's misfortunes were largely due to sloth and immorality. Besides, economic reality decreed that the majority of the world would always be on the troubled side of subsistence. But as industrialization progressed in the nineteenth century, it began to look like machines might lift enormous numbers

Jesse Tarbox Beals
Room in a tenement flat,
1910

Jesse Tarbox Beals
Tenement family making
artificial flowers, ca. 1910

out of poverty, and social and religious thought edged toward considering poverty a social product rather than punishment earned by bad living.[i]

Once the poor were not considered wholly responsible for their own fate, sympathy for them gradually entered consciousness, though for years the lower classes were feared as breeders of disease, crime, possibly even revolution. Still, late in the nineteenth century, two significant developments, the Progressive reform movement and the professionalization of social work, helped make possible the kind of reform campaign that Hine engaged in with his camera from 1906 to 1918 while working for the National Child Labor Committee.

The Progressive reformers, a liberal humanitarian group, built on the relatively new notion that government and the people could control the economy and improve society, and that an informed populace was virtually

Jacob Riis
Bohemian cigarmakers at work in their tenement

certain to do so, for knowledge would move people to act.[ii] The professionalization of social work meant that charity workers emphasized documentation and the systematic amassing of data, creating information banks the Progressives sometimes made use of. Hine's photographic documents, bolstered by detailed field notes that included names, places, dates, ages, heights, and whatever personal and work history he could glean, were meant to provide such irrefutable knowledge of the appalling conditions of child labor that something would be done about it.

Social documentary photography was still in its infancy early in the twentieth century, yet Hine gave it canonical form. Not that he invented it, but his practice and the tenor of his work would influence American documentary photography for decades to come. He considered himself an artist, knew a good deal about art and photography and occasionally made a bow to artistic traditions, but photography was a relatively new medium with new potentials and new demands, and his task had little precedent in the history of art. He pictured a realm that he hoped his own images might obliterate, and he served a social cause at least as faithfully as aesthetics.

Lewis W. Hine
Boys at work in the
Cumberland Glass Works,
Bridgeton, NJ, 1909

His aesthetic sensibility was sophisticated enough, as the Ellis Island pictures in the first decade and the 1930–31 pictures of the construction of the Empire State Building make clear. Some of the child labor pictures exhibit this sophistication, especially when the scene provides a ready-made design, as in the complexities and elegance of a glass factory, the repetitive patterns of broomsticks in a packing room, the geometric jumble of a lumberyard, a girl making lace in a dirty kitchen that looks like a Dutch interior gone bankrupt. But design is not what this work is about. Hine referred to himself as an "interpretative photographer," and in the 1920s a commentator reported that "a picture which has beauty without significance means little to him."[iii]

Although there is no mistaking a trained eye at work in his child labor photographs—it is evident in the careful placements, the multiple light sources, the clever use of perspectives to make factories seem endless—Hine was not always in a position to use his aesthetic skills to maximum effect. A critic was not necessarily welcome in the mills and factories. Occasionally in danger, Hine more than once had to use ruses to get inside, claiming to be a fire inspector, an insurance salesman, a Bible salesman, an industrial photographer. Many of the pictures taken out of doors were taken there simply because he could not get inside.

He had other ruses to ensure that his documentation was accurate, keeping a notebook and pencil in his pocket so he could reach in and make notes without being observed, and he knew the height of his jacket buttons and could secretly measure the children against them. Even when he was less constrained, he did not necessarily put aesthetics first. He was using his art for a cause and to a certain extent was inventing a language as he went, a language that combined documentation and emotional resonance in a grammar of persuasion.

The syntax he adopted was the plainspeak of photography, the kind of humble and reliable reporting the camera comes by naturally and performs faithfully. Many of Hine's pictures have a kind of prosaic matter-of-factness, a flatness and straightforwardness, a head-on recognition of things as they are without need of embellishment, of visible evidence left to speak for itself that turns out to speak more clearly and tellingly than words. He confronts his subjects directly but politely and does not exaggerate, neither prettifying nor emphasizing defects.

Hine's interest in presenting the ills of society as realistically as possible, for the purpose of cleaning them up, was in keeping with the temper of his times. Realism, including critical realism, had a new lease on life in America at that moment. Muckraking journalists like Ida Tarbell and Lincoln Steffens were in full cry. In 1908, The Eight, a group of painters soon known as the Ash Can School because of their impolite focus on back alleys, had their first exhibition. Hine himself spoke of the beauty and essential force of the commonplace at a 1909 meeting of social workers, quoting a passage from *Adam Bede* by George Eliot that urged artists not to neglect work-worn hands, weather-beaten faces, and homes furnished with lowly tin pans. "It is needful," Eliot wrote, "that we should remember their existence, else we may happen to leave them out of our religion and philosophy, and frame lofty theories which only fit a world of extremes. Therefore, let art always remind us of them; therefore, let us always have men ready to give the loving pains of life to the faithful representing of commonplace things, men who see beauty in the commonplace things, and delight in showing how kindly the light of heaven falls on them."[iv]

Lewis W. Hine
Salvin Nocito carrying berries to the bushel man, Browns Mills, NJ, 1910

Because Hine's photographs are so plainspoken, it is sometimes hard to say how *good* a specific picture is, though it is easy enough to judge both the force and value of his extended body of work. Yet Hine's child labor campaign raises the perennial question of how to judge a documentary photograph. Is it good because it meets some criterion of beauty, or does beauty interfere with social messages? Is it good because it tells a story so clearly, so profoundly? Is it good because it made a difference, helped change a bad situation?

There are no simple answers. Hine's photographs are distinguished by a palpable respect for the individual, no matter the age or circumstances, and a strong humanistic concern for all aspects of the person, including situation and personality. His careful, utterly concentrated attention is eminently suited to the camera, as the camera is to his endeavor. Details speak volumes: a boy's broken suspender, a child's bare feet or ill-fitting clothes, the homely order of decaying tenements. These details are background and context, important for the story, necessary for the document. The human being remains crucial, enmeshed in and often overwhelmed by circumstances beyond his or her control but not merely an adjunct, not an appendage to a machine or a statistic in a mill but a particular child—happy, sad, angry, resigned, stubborn, *alive*, usually the center of the picture, obviously the center of the universe as this photographer sees it.

Jacob Riis
Bootblacks and newsboys
shooting craps, 1891

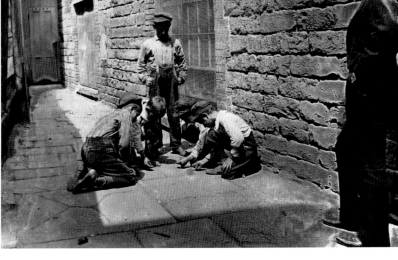

His style formed the basis for American social documentary in the 1930s, when social documentary was in the forefront, and has continued to exert an influence to this day. Ben Shahn, himself a fine documentary photographer in the 1930s, said, "Hine was one of the Greats. I don't know a photographer who has not been conscious of, and influenced to some extent by, Lewis Hine."[v]

Social documentary photography in the service of reform had been pioneered in America by Jacob Riis a mere decade and a half before Hine began work for the National Child Labor Committee. Riis was a journalist who crusaded against the slums that housed the thousands of immigrants streaming into New York from Europe in the last quarter of the nineteenth century. In his autobiography he said, "I wrote, but it seemed to make no impression." He wanted something more convincing than words, could not draw and did not consider drawings adequate evidence anyway. Technology came to his aid. When Riis read about magnesium flash powder in 1887, he

Jacob Riis
Talmud school in a Hester
Street tenement, ca. 1890

realized instantly that flash would make it possible to photograph inside the dark apartments where the urban poor lived their cramped lives. Riis got photographers to assist him and soon learned to handle a camera himself.[vi] His photographs tend to be dark and stamped with strong contrasts because of his flash. Even a picture of a Talmud school that he tried hard to find praise for in words is harrowing in its blackness and the damp that seems to seep from its crumbling walls.

The half-tone reproductive process had only been recently invented, and this too assisted Riis's cause. In 1890, he published *How the Other Half Lives*, the first book to be illustrated (if only in part) by half-tone photographs. It was hugely successful. An older technology, the magic lantern, was even more useful to Riis, who lectured widely, and dramatically, about the scandal of tenement life to middle-class audiences who were stunned by his slides.

The novelty of photographs of the poor and the even greater novelty of Riis's harsh, direct, sometimes brutal images, made an extraordinary impact. Rather than prettying up or sentimentalizing poverty, Riis recorded every bit of clutter, rubbish and grit, every peeling wall, overcrowded bed and tattered garment. He photographed little boys in a pitiless light that threw heavy shadows; he photographed a solemn, uncommonly self-contained little girl with just enough space around her to make her seem woefully isolated. He photographed a boy in a sweatshop and the men behind him from below, throwing everything slightly off kilter. He photographed entire families, parents and children together, working in tight quarters as if their lives depended on it—which they did. In other pictures Riis occasionally tilted the camera or lighted one pitiful figure in an airless gloom or included figures and objects, off at the edges, that photographers ordinarily excluded. The world he depicted was in danger of coming apart, if it did not suffocate first in dirt and misery.

Jacob Riis
"I Scrubs": Little Katie does the housekeeping, cleaning and cooking "of the plain kind"

Jacob Riis
12-year-old boy at work pulling threads in a sweatshop, ca. 1890

Jacob Riis
The Mott Street boys in the
Italian quarter with a keep-
off-the-grass sign,
ca. 1890

Unfamiliar subjects, depicted in an unfamiliar technique and in a style that had no precedents the audience could call upon: Riis arrived at a moment when people had never seen photographs of the kind of poverty and crowding he hoped to crush, much less photographs as rough and disorienting as the ones he took. He invited shock. We who are so accustomed to worse can scarcely understand how powerful the novelty of these images was. Sometimes people were so shaken they cried or even fainted.[vii] They also changed the tenement laws. Riis was immensely effective.

Jacob Riis
Minding the baby,
ca. 1898

Photography of social ills, so new when Riis started his crusade, increased in a few years as the hand-held camera, faster lenses and magnesium flash made some subjects more accessible. By the end of the 1890s, half-tone reproduction had put photographic illustrations into many magazines and to a more limited extent into newspapers, so that photographs of all kinds were much more commonly available to the public than they had been before. In 1909, Hine could say to a social work audience, "Perhaps you are weary of child labor pictures. Well, so are the rest of us, but we propose to make you and the whole country so sick and tired of the whole business that when the time for action comes, child labor pictures will be records of the past."[viii] Ten years earlier, it would have been absurd for Riis to suggest his audience might be tired of photographs like his.

Riis's photographic career and Hine's overlapped slightly. Riis gave up photography at the beginning of the century—his 1914 obituary did not even note the fact that he had been a photographer—but he continued to lecture, and both his books and his reforms lived on. Hine never once mentioned him in print. Did he consider Riis too sensationalistic to be trusted? The expanding realm of photography had affected the public's attitudes to the medium in a few short years. Even as Riis crusaded, the yellow press was stirring up the Spanish-American war, faking some photographs, leaning ever more heavily on sensational

Jacob Riis
"Rushing the growler
[beer can]," ca. 1898

Jacob Riis
Little Susie at work in
Gotham Court, ca. 1890

topics. The nineteenth century's burning belief in photography started to dim ever so slightly. By 1908, when Hine went to work full time for the NCLC, he felt he had to guard against a distrust that had not been there in Riis's day, one major reason why Hine documented everything so carefully and included a witness whenever possible.

Of course his personality was also different from Riis's. Hine was an educator. Born in Wisconsin in 1874, he first worked in a furniture store and knocked about from job to job for a while, trying his hand at sculpture. His first real career, beginning in 1901, was teaching at the Ethical Culture School in New York City, and soon he took a graduate degree at the Columbia University School of Social Work in New York. It was because Hine was asked to be the school photographer at Ethical Culture that he picked up a camera, and, learning as he went, set up a darkroom and an after-school camera club. In 1908, Paul Strand was one of his students.

Frank Manny, the school Superintendent and in many ways Hine's mentor, already understood that photographs could change minds. In 1904, he and Hine went to Ellis Island to photograph arriving immigrants. Manny believed, as did Hine, that the current generation of immigrants, who inspired fear and disdain among those who had arrived here earlier, deserved both sympathy and respect, and that photographs of them could influence people's attitudes. Hine had been educating children; now he set about educating adult minds. In mid-1908, when he left the school to accept a full-time position with the NCLC, he said, "I felt that I was merely changing my educational efforts from the classroom to the world."[ix]

America, and much of the industrialized world, was experiencing a major cultural change, both in the nature of child labor and in attitudes toward it. For centuries, it had been the norm for children to work beside their parents. With the advent of the industrial revolution, work had become more dangerous, yet children were increasingly sought out by manufacturers who paid them so little that the competition forced adults to accept lower wages. In the later nineteenth century, Americans heard how bad the conditions were from journalists; uneasiness stirred. In 1870, the census recorded child laborers for the first time. In 1872, the Prohibition party platform condemned child labor.[x]

In 1906, the introduction to *The Bitter Cry of the Children*, John Spargo's book on the plight of the poverty-stricken young, remarked on what we now call compassion fatigue: "The appeal of adults in poverty is an old appeal, so old indeed that we have become in a measure hardened to its pathos and insensitive to its tragedy. But this book represents the cry of the child in distress, and it will touch every human heart and even arouse to action the stolid and apathetic."[xi] Riis had already given an account of child labor in pictures of children doing piecework at home. Awareness of the problem was no longer the issue. Indifference and apathy were.

At the same time, a new kind of attention was being focused on children. The birthrate was declining, raising concern about the welfare of future generations and fears that impoverished children would become damaged citizens. New ideas about child development were also in the air, evident in the institution of progressive education, playgrounds, and juvenile courts, as well as a heightened emotional investment in children and a breakdown of the traditional valuation of them as part of the family's economic support.[xii] The National Child Labor Committee, born under the pressure of all these forces in 1904, hired Hine as a free-lance in 1906 and a full-time staff member in 1908.

The NCLC understood and utilized all available means of persuasion. In its first year of operation it published repeatedly and extensively on child labor as well as managing to place articles in the papers, and in the following years its publications increased.[xiii] Late in the nineteenth century, advertising had grown prodigiously; the importance of publicity in the modern era was unmistakable. At a conference of social workers in 1909, one speaker advised the audience to borrow the techniques of advertisers: "The rule of right publicity in public health work, as I see it, is essentially the same as the rule for commercial advertising: as striking as you can make it."[xiv]

The NCLC was the first organization to use photographs consistently and extensively in an effort to bring about change. They picked the right man for the job.

Hine was indefatigable. Sometimes he traveled as much as 50,000 miles a year by car and train; eventually he took more than 5,000 photographs for the Committee. Over the years he photographed in Southern mills, in glass factories, fish canneries, mines, on urban streets with news vendors and messengers, in the fields with cotton and berry pickers, in tenements, in New York, New Jersey, Connecticut, Rhode Island, Massachusetts, Vermont, Pennsylvania, Indiana, Ohio, Delaware, Maryland, West Virginia, North Carolina, South Carolina, Georgia, Mississippi, Louisiana, Missouri, everywhere he found a child at work who ought to be in school or out playing in the few years life allots to play.

Hine carried with him about 50 pounds of equipment, including a 5 x 7 box-type view camera. He was highly visible, which accounts for the fact that so many of his subjects were looking directly at him; he could scarcely steal their pictures. His mission was to register facts clearly—and it is a remarkable accomplishment that he recorded such a variety of circumstances, so many groups, so many settings, so much mechanical and random information, such injustice and such supposedly un-formed personalities while still making room for feeling and still allowing his subjects' humanity to shine forth. The director of the NCLC would later say that Hine was "the first person to focus the camera intelligently, sympathetically, and effectively on social work problems," which previously had been "intellectually but not emotionally recognized."[xv]

Typically Hine's composition puts the child or children front and center; the surrounding

Lewis W. Hine
Small newsie downtown,
St. Louis, MO, 1910

space is background or pivots around the central figure, revealing the workplace or machine or task the child is involved with. The American attitude toward the machine was highly ambivalent then; Henry Adams Jr. thought the dynamo might be an object of worship, but many feared the dehumanizing aspect of mechanical labor. The machines in Hine's pictures are stunningly different from the backgrounds in children's portraits in Hine's day: Mary Cassatt's and Gertrude Käsebier's domestic interiors with mothers paying close attention to their babies, studio portraits of tots dressed up within an inch of their lives, newly popular home snapshots of youngsters on the front porch, togged out in clean clothes and looking perplexed.

The child laborers introduce an organic element into the perfected world of machines, those identical gears and rows of bobbins that take up all the available space and dwarf the imperfect human forms up front. The children's fragility is accentuated by nondescript dresses, messy hair, narrow limbs and bare feet; even when a boy strikes a pose of mastery he is clearly too small to fill it. The handsome mechanical elements, so much better constructed than the young laborers, tell pointed tales about what controls and dominates the young lives in these pictures.

Hine sometimes pulls back to survey the factory and make the situation all too clear. The sharp perspectives racing to the center of the frame make the mills seem even longer than they are and the children even smaller; at times the machinery seems to be advancing on us. When the children are regularly spaced over the length of the workplace they become a kind of mechanical accessory themselves.

They pose, as might be expected when a man's camera cannot be concealed, or a very young child may turn around to look at the strange man while her elders work. At times the superintendent or manager poses with his young employees. What were the bosses thinking? Many owners believed, or had convinced themselves, that impoverished families needed their children's pitiful incomes, so employing underage workers was doing them a service. Hine's portraits do opt for pathos or sadness some of the time, but sorrow, after all, is part of the point. So is the adult look that some of these youngsters wear long before they deserve to.

Most of Hine's subjects had probably never had their pictures taken before; his portraits provide a primer of camera behavior among a new population. Often the children are stiff, even rigid, as if turning themselves into daguerreotypes—or machines—and most are solemn, utterly serious, occasionally forlorn. In groups you can see different ways of confronting the camera and wonderfully varied expressions—shy, aggressive, confident, amused—and boys will sometimes show off for one another, even strike macho poses, or exhibit a weary bravado, mouthing a cigar. Some children smile as cameras eventually made everyone do, and a six-year-old berry picker flirts outrageously with the man who will immortalize her.

Hine refused to sensationalize a state of affairs that was shameful on its face, though his pictures of blackened boys in mines are shocking enough. He did welcome irony when it came ready-made. A sad little newsboy hawks his wares ignored by well-fed and well-clothed passersby. Another, very young, smiles on the steps of a trolley car as if he were stepping out for a day at the zoo. A line of too-young newsboys poses before the mighty capitol of a nation that hasn't bothered to make their employment illegal.

Hine was willing too, to allow life and its surprises into the picture. Two boys who have been picking a dump laugh with one another, though you might think there was nothing to laugh about. In a tenement a working family, overpowered by the space above them, concentrates on their labor, while a baby in a corner of the frame suddenly looks up at the camera, at us. Commentators have pointed out that Hine's pictures of families seldom include fathers, making the mother and children seem more needy still.

Hine fervently believed in the effectiveness of pictures, and of his pictures. He told a group of social workers that if a picture of "a tiny spinner" was combined with a sympathetically written caption, "What a lever we have for the social uplift." In that same speech he said that a picture "is often more effective than the reality would have been, because, in the picture, the non-essential and conflicting interests have been eliminated....The photograph has an added realism of its own; it has an inherent attraction not found in other forms of illustration."[xvi]

Lewis W. Hine
Boys picking over garbage on "the dumps," Boston, MA, 1909

He also found and organized more extensive ways to use photographs, making photography a prime and widely varied means of communication and persuasion. By 1909 he controlled the design and layout of his pictures and captions, put together pamphlets, posters and exhibitions for the NCLC, gave slide lectures and prepared sets of slides for rent with typewritten manuscripts from the Committee. In 1914 alone, 11 exhibits were organized and shown in 50 cities in 20 states, as well as in 16 different places in New York City.[xvii] The posters had such messages as "Making Human Junk," "The Normal Child" compared to "The Mill Child," "Accidents...And so they pay with a maimed life," and "Moral Dangers," which meant newsboys who worked late at night carrying notes to jails or saloons or prostitutes. Hine's investigation of photography's multiple roles as a messenger was an important step along the medium's route into more and more areas of everyday life.

He played yet another role in photographic history: as a precursor of the photo essay, a form that was not fully developed until the 1930s. Hine thought of pictures as "tell(ing) a story packed into the most condensed and vital form,"[xviii] and his combination of words and pictures, sometimes in sequences—see especially the survey of Pittsburgh's working community in 1909—began to organize photographs to tell stories that were not simple chronological progressions.

The cumulative effect of Hine's child labor photographs was highly effective, if ultimately not effective enough. The documents he presented could not be denied by the manufacturers and other people who had been so sure that conditions could not be as bad as the reformers claimed. Hine's work reinforced the Progressive credo, that informed people will be moved to action. It offered evidence as well for some home truths about the persuasive value of photography: photographs can be highly effective propaganda, but they not only cannot work alone, requiring immense amounts of cooperation on the part of language, distribution, and a public ready to be convinced, but they are probably no better than other media at bucking the tides of history. The NCLC helped make a number of inroads on the child labor problem, yet America was not prepared to write a national law until years later.

The Committee was not initially in favor of a federal law but hoped to encourage the passage of new state regulations and laws that had teeth, and to spur enforcement of existing local laws that were generally ignored. The country did begin to move, if sluggishly, against child labor even before Hine played a major role in the campaign. In 1906, a proposal for a national law was introduced in Congress but did not pass. But by 1912, 34 states had new laws or had amended existing laws, and though the South had been the most recalcitrant section of the country, every Southern state had a child labor law on its books. And that year, the government created a U.S. Children's Bureau.

Yet there was much more improvement on paper than in fact. In 1900, the national census recorded that 18.2 percent of children between the ages of 10 and 15 were working; in 1910 the percentage was 18.4.[xix] Still, the issue of children's welfare, and particularly of child labor, was on the table, and the nation was debating it. In 1916, Congress passed a national child labor law; in 1918, the Supreme Court declared it unconstitutional. In 1924, Congress attempted to write a child labor amendment to the Constitution, but the South was opposed, and the states never ratified it. It was not until 1938 that a child labor law became the law of the land, in the Fair Labor Standards Act. By then Hine, who had left the NCLC in 1918 and gone on to other projects, could scarcely find work and was nearly impoverished. He died in 1940.

The problems were not over then and are not now. In 1999 the United Nations estimated that more than a quarter of a million children 14 or under were currently working somewhere in the world.[xx] In June of that year, the International Labor Organization adopted a treaty meant to wipe off the world's record the worst forms of child labor but not to ban the labor of children. In the last few years, the Western world has rather suddenly discovered that many of its favorite name-brand clothes and running shoes are manufactured in Asian countries by child laborers. Pressure has been brought to bear on the manufacturers, but the problems are no simpler now than they were in Hine's day. In countries where for centuries child labor was necessary to keep the family alive parents and authorities often believe work is essential, education a luxury, and the country too poor to educate its poorer children anyway. This idea is belied by African countries that, despite lower per capita incomes, have been more successful at educating their populace than countries with greater resources. The challenge is to convince people that children's education will contribute more, over time, to the family's welfare than the pittance they earn when small.[xxi]

But it is not only in poor and underdeveloped countries that children do the work of adults. In 1999 in the United States, Sears was fined for allowing 16- and 17-year-old employees to operate power-driven equipment in violation of child-labor laws.[xxii] That same year, Italy reported that more than 130,000 children dropped out of school each year to work full time, and that child labor was rising. An influx of immigrants had contributed to this problem, as was doubtless the case elsewhere. And Italy had a new problem surely not exclusive to that country: children who were not poverty stricken now worked to buy themselves the latest brand of sneakers, the hottest video game.[xxiii]

Even children have organized against child labor. In 1995, when he was only 12, a Canadian boy named Craig Kielburger, appalled by a story in the paper, started a small club called Free the Children as a means to fight child labor practices across the world.

By 1999 his club received approximately $300,000 a year and had helped pressure the Canadian and Italian governments to stiffen laws against adults who employed child prostitutes and to convince Nike to bar anyone under age 16 from its factories. Kielburger obviously knows the power of pictures: when he lectures to school children and others, he shows slides of child workers in many countries.[xxiv]

The world has turned a number of times since Hine walked into the mills with a camera, but the Progressive idea lives on, for a teenage boy has moved adults and adolescents to action with an information campaign, and the social documentary photography that Hine made such a powerful instrument lives on at the hands of other photographers.

Notes

i   See Robert H. Bremner, *From the Depths: The Discovery of Poverty in the United States* (New York: New York University Press, 1956), pp. 3–30.

ii   See Verna Posever Curtis and Stanley Mallach, *Photography and Reform: Lewis Hine and the National Child Labor Committee*, Milwaukee Art Museum, 1984, pp. 10, 17.

iii   "A Camera Interpretation of Labor," *The Mentor* 14 (September 1926), p. 43; cited by Miles Orvell, "Lewis Hine: The Art of the Commonplace," *History of Photography*, v. 16, no. 2 (Summer, 1992), p. 87.

iv   Lewis W. Hine, "Social Photography; How the Camera May Help in the Social Uplift," in *Proceedings of the National Conference of Charities and Corrections*, 1909, ed. Alexander Johnson (Fort Wayne, Ind.: Press of Fort Wayne Printing Co.), p. 339.

v   Quoted as the epigraph to *Lewis W. Hine and the American Social Conscience* by Judith Mara Gutman (New York: Walker and Company, 1967).

vi   Jacob A. Riis, *The Making of an American* (New York: The Macmillan Company, 1901), pp. 266–269.

vii   See Peter Bacon Hales, *Silver Cities: The Photography of American Urbanization, 1839–1915* (Philadelphia: Temple University Press, 1984), p. 193.

viii   Lewis W. Hine, "Social Photography," *op. cit.*, p. 356.

ix   Russell Freedman, *Kids at Work: Lewis Hine and the Crusade Against Child Labor* (New York: Clarion Books, 1994), p. 19. Unfortunately, the book has no source notes whatsoever.

x   Walter I. Trattner, *Crusade for the Children: A History of the National Child Labor Committee and Child Labor Reform in America* (Chicago: Quadrangle Books, 1970), p. 32.

xi   Robert Hunter, in *Spargo* (New York: Garrett Press, 1970, originally published by The Macmillan Company, 1906), p. viii.

xii   See Curtis and Mallach, *Photography and Reform*, *op. cit.*, p. 16, and Myron Weiner, *The Child and the State in India: Child Labor and Education Policy in Comparative Perspective* (Princeton, N. J.: Princeton University Press, 1991), p. 110.

xiii   Trattner, *Crusade for the Children, op. cit.*, p. 75.

xiv   John A. Kingsbury, "Right Publicity and Public Health Work," *Proceedings of the National Conference of Charities and Corrections*, 1909, *op. cit.*, p. 333.

xv   Owen Lovejoy, "Hail to Hine," *Survey* 63 (Nov. 15, 1929), pp. 236–7; cited by Maren Stange, *Symbols of Ideal Life*, p. 66.

xvi   Lewis W. Hine, "Social Photography," *op. cit.*, p. 356.

xvii   *Child Labor Bulletin III*, no. 3, November 1914, pp. 16–17; cited by Stephen Victor, "Lewis Hine's Photography and Reform in Rhode Island," *Rhode Island History*, vol. 41, no. 2, May 1982, pp. 41–42.

xviii   Lewis W. Hine, "Social Photography," *op. cit.*, p. 356.

xix   See Trattner, *Crusade for the Children, op. cit.*, pp. 65–66, 87, 98, 107.

xx   See Steven Greenhouse, "A Crusade of Children," *New York Times*, April 17, 1999, p. B1.

xxi   Myron Weiner, *The Child and the State in India, op. cit.*, p. 3.

xxii   Steven Greenhouse, "Sears Is Fined $325,000 by U.S. For Violating Child-Labor Laws," *New York Times*, May 16, 1999.

xxiii   Rachel Donadio, "Child Labor Is Said to Be on Rise in Italy," *Italy Daily (Corriere della Sera)* April 16, 1999, p. 1.

xxiv   Greenhouse, "A Crusade of Children."

CHILDREN AT WORK: THEIR MANY FACES

Young cigarmakers in Engelhardt & Company. Three boys looked under 14. Work was slack and youngsters were not being employed much. Labor leaders told me in busy times many small boys and girls were employed. Youngsters all smoke. Tampa, Fla., Jan. 27, 1909.

Mendicants. New York City, July 1910.

Boys picking over garbage on "the dumps." Boston, Mass., Oct. 1909.

Joseph Severio, peanut vendor, 11 years of age. Been pushing cart 2 years.
Out after midnight, on May 21, 1910. Ordinarily works 6 hours per day.
Works of own volition. Doesn't smoke, all earnings go to father.
Wilmington, Del., May 1910.

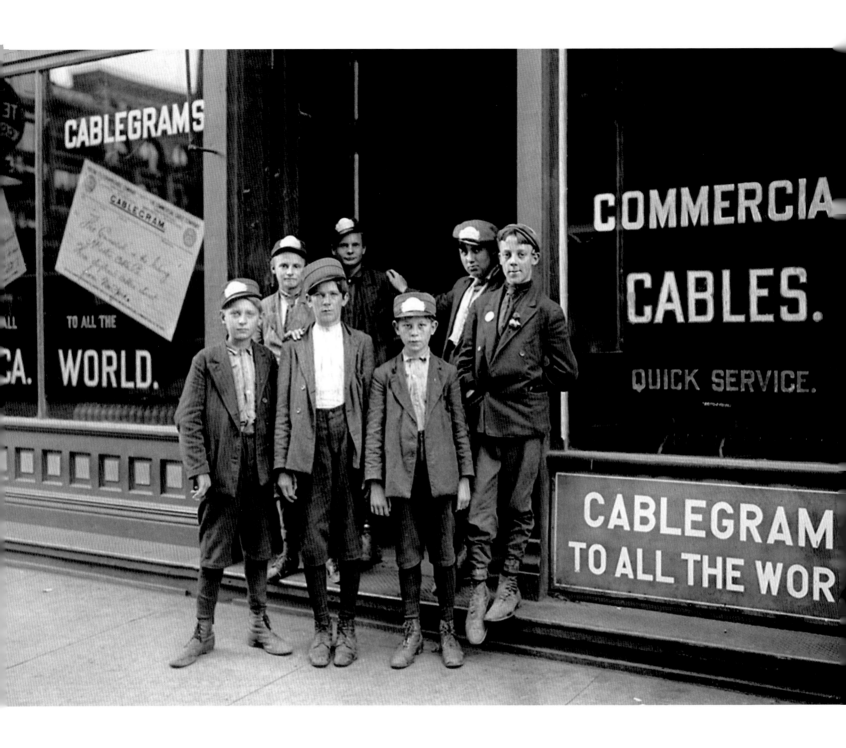

Postal Telegraph Messengers. (Indiana has no age limit for messengers).
Indianapolis, Ind., Aug. 1908.

A typical group of Postal Messengers. Smallest on left end, Wilmore
Johnson, been there for one year. Works days only. The postal boys are
not nearly so young in Norfolk and also other Va. cities, as are the Western
Union Boys. Norfolk, Va., June 1911.

Getting working papers. New York, Feb. 10, 1908.

Boys making melon baskets. A basket factory. Evansville, Ind., Oct. 1908.

Boys in packing room, Brown Mfg. company. Evansville, Ind., Oct. 1908.

Bowery bootblack. New York City, July 1910.

Marie Costa, Basket Seller, in a Cincinnati Market. 10 A.M. Saturday.
Cincinnati, Ohio, Aug. 22, 1908.

After 9 P.M. 7-year-old Tommie Nooman demonstrating the advantages of
the Ideal Necktie Form in store window on Pennsylvania Ave., Washington,
D.C. His father said, "He is the youngest demonstrator in America.
Has been doing it for several years from San Francisco, to New York.
We stay a month or six weeks in a place, he works at it off and on." The
remarks of appreciation from the by-standers were not having the best
effect on Tommie. Washington, D.C., April 13, 1911.

Young boy working for Hickok Lumber Co. Burlington, Vt., Sept. 2, 1910.

Three families is the rule of these shacks, one room above and one below,
but sometimes four families crowd in. Outdoor dining room at side.
Maryland, July 7, 1909.

Making dresses for Campbell kids dolls in a dirty tenement. The older boy about 12 years old, operates the machine when the mother is not using it, and when she is using it, he helps the little ones break the threads. New York City, March 11, 1912.

A load of kimonos just finished, girl very reticent. New York City, Feb. 10, 1912.

Home of Mrs. Schiaffo. She is a contractor, getting lace from the home workers in the neighborhood. (Woman in black has just brought in some work) and the lace goes to a manufacturing company. On the couch with Mrs. S. is 7-year-old Willie, who is learning to make lace. New York City, Dec. 21, 1911.

Camela, 12 years old, making Irish lace for collars. Works until 9 P.M. in dirty kitchen. New York City, Jan. 27, 1912.

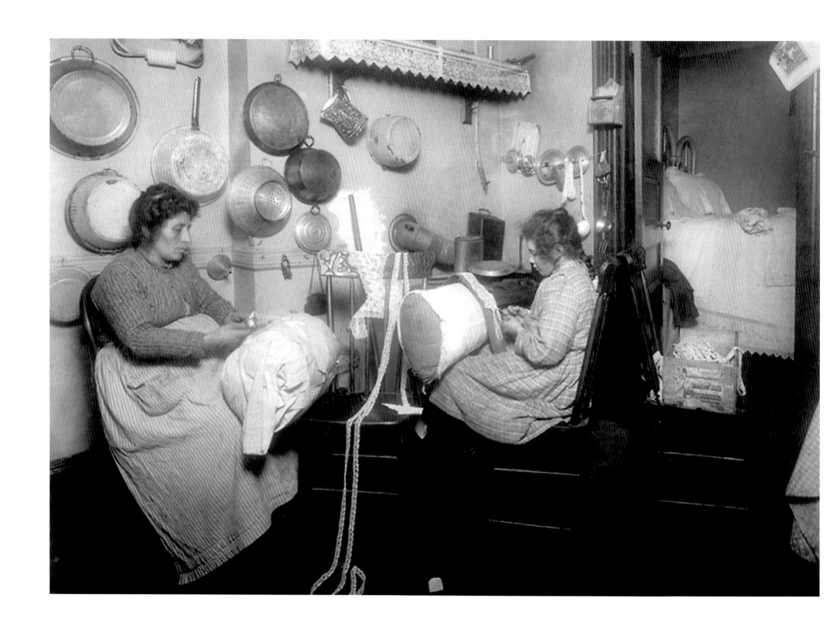

Mrs. Palontona and 13-year-old daughter, working on pillow lace in dirty kitchen of their tenement home. They were both very illiterate. Mother is making fancy lace and girl sold me the lace she worked on. New York City, Dec. 22, 1911.

Malestestra. Get 6¢ a gross and make regularly from 10 to 12 gross a day. Mr. Malestestra has been ill for 2 years, and can do no heavy work. But makes artificial flowers all day. Mr. Malestestra helps because health too bad to work out. Mrs. Malestestra, Frank, age 14, John, age 11, Lizzie age 4. Boys work on Saturday, afternoons and evenings till 10 or 11. Lizzie separates petals. New York City, Jan. 5, 1908.

Family of Mrs. Motto making flowers in a dirty tenement. Josephine,
13 years, helps outside of school hours until 9 P.M. sometimes. She is soon
to be 14 and expects to go to work in an embroidery factory, then. Says
she worked in that factory all last summer. All work, except baby and he
plays with the flowers putting them together and they expect him to work
before long. Father drives a coach or a hack irregularly. New York City,
Dec. 15, 1911.

A family picking nuts. Mother nursing baby while picking nuts. Was suffering with a sore throat. Rosie, 3, hanging around; Genevieve, 6, Tessie, 6, picks too. Make $1.50 to $2 a week. New York City, Dec. 13, 1911.

POUNDING THE PAVEMENT: THE NEWSIES

Amusing themselves while waiting for morning papers. New York City,
Feb. 11, 1908.

In comparison with governmental affairs, newsies are small matters. This photo was taken in the shadow of where the laws are made. This group of young newsboys sell on the Capitol grounds every day, ages 8, 9, 10, 11, 12, the only boy with a badge was 8 years old. Washington, D.C., April 10, 1912.

Newsboy and newsgirl. Getting afternoon papers. New York City,
July 1910.

High school route boys. Adolescents. Some in back row have been newsboys for seven, eight and nine years. New Haven, Conn., March 8, 1909.

After midnight selling extras. There were many young boys selling very late
these nights. Youngest boy in the group is 9 years old. Harry, 11 years old,
Eugene and the rest were a little older. Washington, D.C., April 17, 1912.

Francis Lance, 5 years old, 41 inches high. He jumps on and off moving
cars at risk of life. St. Louis, Mo., May 1910.

Small newsie downtown. Saturday afternoon. St. Louis, Mo.,
May 7, 1910.

Joe Smith, 8 years old. St. Louis, Mo., May 1910.

One of the young spinners in the Quidwick Co. Mill (a Polish boy, Willie)
who was taking his noon rest in a doffer box. Anthony, R.I., April 16, 1909.

Addie Laird, 12 years old. Spinner in a Cotton Mill. Girls in mill say
she is 10 years old. She admitted to me that she was 12 years old, that
she started during school vacation and would now stay. North Pownal,
Vt., Feb. 9, 1910.

General view of spinning room, Cornell Mill. Fall River, Mass., Jan. 11/12,
ca. 1908.

The overseer said apologetically, "She just happened in." She was working steadily when the investigator found her. The mills seem full of youngsters who "just happened in" or "are helping sister." Newberry, S.C., Dec. 1908.

Some adolescents in Bibb Mfg. Co. Macon, Ga., Jan. 19, 1909.

At machine in Stanislaus, Beauvais has worked in spinning room for two
years. Salem, Mass., Oct. 26, 1911.

Sadie Pfeifer, 48 inches high. Has worked half a year. One of the many
small children at work in Lancaster Cotton Mills. Lancaster, S.C., Nov. 30,
1908.

Rhodes Mfg. Co. spinner. A moment's glimpse of the outer world.
Said she was 11 years old. Been working over a year. Lincolnton, N.C.,
Nov. 11, 1908.

Bibb Mill No. 1, Macon, Ga. Many youngsters here. Some boys and girls were so small they had to climb up on to the spinning frame to mend broken threads and to put back the empty bobbins. Macon, Ga., Jan. 19, 1909.

Boy at warping machine in Newton Cotton Mill. Been there 2 years.
Newton, S.C., Dec. 21, 1908.

Some of the doffers and the Supt. Ten small boys and girls about this
size out of a force of 40 employees. Catawba Cotton Mill. Newton, N.C.,
Dec. 21, 1908.

Spinner in Vivian Cotton Mills. Been at it 2 years. Where will her good
looks be in 10 years? Cherryville, N.C., Nov. 10, 1908.

One of the spinners in the Whitnel Cotton Mill. She was 51 inches high. Has been in the mill one year. Sometimes works at night. Runs 4 sides— 48¢ a day. When asked how old she was, she hesitated, then said, "I don't remember," then confidentially, "I'm not old enough to work, but do just the same." Out of 50 employees, ten children about her size. Whitnel, N.C., Dec. 22, 1908.

Furman Owens, 12 years old. Can't read. Doesn't know ABCs.
"Yes, I want to learn, but can't when I work all the time." Been in mills
4 years, 3 years in Olympia Mill. Columbia, S.C., Jan. 16, 1909.

Closing hour, Saturday noon, at Dallas Mill. Every child in photo, so far as
I was able to ascertain, works in that mill. When I questioned some of the
boys as to their ages, they said they were 12, and then other boys said they
were lying. (Which sentiment I agreed to.). Huntsville, Ala., Nov. 19, 1910.

Sweeper and doffer boys in Lancaster Cotton Mills. Many more as small.
Lancaster, S.C., Dec. 1, 1908.

Spinners and doffers in Lancaster Cotton Mills. Dozens of them in this
mill. Lancaster, S.C., Dec. 1, 1908.

Jo Bodeon, a back-roper in mule room. Chace Cotton Mill. Burlington, Vt.,
May 7, 1909.

Workers in the Tifton Cotton Mills. All these children were working or
helping. 125 workers in all. Some of the smallest boys and girls have been
there one year or more. Tifton, Ga., Jan. 22, 1909.

Eddie Norton, a sweeper in Saxon Hill. Spartanburg, S.C., May 17, 1912.

COAL MINERS

Breaker boys working in Ewen Breaker. S. Pittston, Pa., Jan. 10, 1911.

Young Driver in Mine. Has been driving one year. 7 A.M. to 5:30 P.M. daily in Brown Mine. Brown, W. Va., Sept. 1908.

A lonely job. Waiting all alone in the dark for a trip to come through.
It was so damp that Willie said he had to be doctoring all the time for his
cough. A short distance from here the gas was pouring in so rapidly that it
made a great torch when the foreman lit it. Willie has been working here for
4 months 500 feet down the shaft. Walls have been whitewashed to make it
lighter.

Jan. 16 I found Willie at home sick. His mother admitted he is only 13
years old, will be 14 next July. She said that 4 months ago the mine boss
told the father to take Willie to work, and they obtained a certificate from
Squire Barrett. (The only thing the squire could do was to make Willie out
to be 16 years old.) Willie's father and brothers are miners, and the home is
that of a frugal German family. South Pittston, Pa., Jan. 7, 1911.

At the close of the day. Just up from the shaft. All work below ground in Shaft #6 Pennsylvania Coal Co. Clement Tiskie, (smallest boy next to righthand end) is a nipper. Arthur Havard (on Clement's right hand) is a driver. Jo Puma (on Arthur's right) is a nipper. Jo's mother showed me the passport which shows Jo to be 14 years old but he has no school certificate although working inside the mine. Frank Fleming (boy on left of photo), a nipper. Works a mile underground from the shaft which is 500 ft. down. South Pittston, Pa., Jan. 6, 1911.

Three young boys with shovels standing in doorway of a Fort Worth &
Denver train car.

Breaker #9, Hughestown Borough Pa. Coal Co. One of these is James
Leonard, another is Stanley Rasmus. Pittston, Pa., Jan. 16, 1911.

Glass blower and mold boy. Boy has 4½ hours of this at a stretch,
then an hour's rest and 4½ more: cramped position. Day shift one week:
night shift next. Grafton, W. Va., Oct. 1908.

Rob Kidd, one of the young workers, Glass Factory. Alexandria, Va.,
June 23, 1911.

9 P.M. in an Indiana Glass Works. Indiana, Aug. 1908.

Two of the boys on night shift in the More, Jonas Glass Co. Bridgeton,
N.J., Nov. 16, 1909.

Noon hour at Obear-Nestor Glass Co. All these boys are working at the
glass works. St. Louis, Mo., May 10, 1910.

Indiana Glass Works. Midnight. Indiana, Aug. 1908.

Cumberland Glass Works. A young holding mold boy is seen, dimly, in the middle distance to left of center. Negroes, Greeks, Italians are being employed in many glass houses. Bridgeton, N.J., Nov. 15, 1909.

Day scene. Wheaton Glass Works. Boy is Howard Lee. His mother showed me the family record in Bible which gave birth July 15, 1894. 15 years old now but has been in glass works two years and some nights. Started at 13 years old. Millville, N.J., Nov. 1909.

Laura Petty, a 6-year-old berry picker on Jenkins Farm.
"I'm just beginnin'. Picked two boxes yesterday." Gets 2¢ a box.
Rock Creek, Md., July 7, 1909.

Norris Luvitt, been picking 3 years in berry fields near Baltimore.
July 8, 1909.

Boy who carries barrels. Robert Saunders, 10 years old. Is the son of the
boss. Mother picks too. Falmouth, Mass., Sept. 20, 1911.

Alberta McNadd on Chester Truitt's Farm. Alberta is 5 years old, and has been picking berries since she was 3. Her mother volunteered the information that she picks from sun-up to sun-down. Cannon, Del., May 28, 1910.

The girl berry carriers on Newton's Farm. Ann Parion 13 years of age working her 5th season, carries 60 lbs. of berries from the fields to the sheds. Andenito Carro, 14 years old, working her 2nd season is seen carrying a 25 lb. load of berries. Besides the great physical strain in carrying such weight, these girls also pick berries. When Andenito was asked her age she responded 12, at which her mother interrupted to say she was past 14. Cannon, Del., May 28, 1910.

Salvin Nocito, 5 years old, carries 2 pecks of cranberries for long distance
to the bushel man. Whites Bog. Browns Mills, N.J., September 28, 1910.

Charlie Ferande showing the scoop with which he works. Most of the
scooping is done by adults. Wareham, Mass., Sept. 13, 1911.

Young pickers on Swift's Bog. All working. Falmouth, Mass.,
Sept. 20, 1911.

All these are shrimp pickers. Youngest in photo are 5 and 8 years old.
Biloxi, Miss., Feb. 20, 1911.

Manuel the young shrimp picker, 5 years old and a mountain of
oyster shells behind him. He worked last year. Understands not a word of
English. Biloxi, Miss., Feb. 20, 1911.

Johnnie, a nine-year-old oyster shucker. Man with pipe is a padrone who
has brought these people from Baltimore for four years. He said, "I tell you
I have to lie to 'em. They're never satisfied. Hard work to get them." He is
the boss of the shucking shed. Dunbar, La., Mar. 2, 1911.

All these boys are cutters in a Canning Co. Ages range from 7 to 12.
They live near the factory. 7-year-old boy in front, Byron Hamilton, has a
badly cut finger but helps his brother regularly. Behind him is his brother
George, 11 years old. He cut his finger half off while working. They and
many youngsters said they were always cutting themselves. George earns a
$1 some days usually 75¢. Some of the others say they earn $1 when they
work all day. At times they start at 7 A.M. work all day until midnight, but
the work is very irregular. Eastport, Me., August 12, 1911.

Some of the cartoners, not the youngest, at Seacoast Canning Co. Eastport,
Me., August 17, 1911.

Butcher knife used by Ralph, a young cutter in a Canning Factory, and
a badly cut finger. Several children working with him had cut fingers, and
even the adults said they could not help cutting themselves. Eastport, Me.,
Aug. 14, 1911.

Minnie Thomas, 9 years old, showing the average size of the sardine
knife as large as this. Minnie works regularly, mostly in the packing room,
and when very busy works nights. Cuts some, also cartons. She says she
earns $2 some days packing. Eastport, Me., Aug. 17, 1911.

"I nearly cut my finger off, cutting sardines the other day." 7-year-old
Byron. Eastport, Me., Aug. 1911.

Lewis W. Hine, ca. 1903

1874   Lewis Wickes Hine is born September 26 to Sarah Hayes Hine and Douglas Hull, operator of a coffee shop and restaurant, in Oshkosh, Wisconsin.

1892   Hine graduates from high school. Starts working in an upholstery factory after his father is killed in an accident. Earns $4 for a 13-hour, six-day workweek.

1892–1900   Works in a clothing store, water filter company, and as "supervising sweeper" in a bank. Studies stenography, drawing, and sculpture. Gets to know Frank A. Manny, professor of Education and Psychology at the State Normal School, who is interested in modern teaching methods.

1900   Studies teaching at the University of Chicago at Manny's suggestion.

1901   Moves to New York with Manny. Engaged as assistant teacher of nature study and geography at the Ethical Culture School in New York. Attends the School of Education at New York University.

1902   Hine's mother dies in Oshkosh.

1903   Manny suggests that Hine start learning photography. Hine photographs school events, teaches students to take photos, and starts a photography club.

1904   Marries the teacher Sarah Ann Rich. Starts the photo project "Ellis Island" with Manny, which uses photos to teach the public about immigrants to counterbalance negative sentiments about them.

1905   Receives a Pd.M. degree in education from New York University.

1906   Starts publishing articles about the value of photography in education. Works as a professional sociological photographer in addition to his teaching job. Starts to work for the National Child Labor Committee (NCLC) on a freelance basis.

1907   Assigned to document New York Tenement Homework for the NCLC. Studies sociology at the Graduate School of Arts and Sciences, Columbia University, where he gets to know Arthur and Paul Kellogg, who worked as editors for the periodical *Charities and the Commons* (later renamed *The Survey* and then *Survey Graphic*). Assigned by Paul Kellogg to take photographs for the Pittsburgh Survey, a sociological study to promote rational understanding of social and economic inequities in industrial cities.

1908   Gives up his teaching job to concentrate fully on photography. Employed full-time by the NCLC to document child labor. Hine's photos are used in newspaper articles, NCLC publications, on posters, and for publicity.

1909   Travels to Georgia, Connecticut, New England, Maryland, New Jersey, and North Carolina to document child labor conditions. Works as staff photographer for *The Survey* and provides photo essays and takes photographs for the New York State Immigrant Commission (Chairman, Louis Marshall).

1910–11   Travels throughout the country for the NCLC; also attends meetings of the NCLC to explain the use of photographs in the fight against child labor.

1912   Son, Corydon, is born. Buys land in Hastings-on-Hudson, New York, for a future home.

1913–14   Named head of the NCLC's exhibition department. Travels to take photographs and to lecture for the NCLC.

1917   Moves to Hastings-on-Hudson with his family. Stops working for the NCLC because of a decision to lower his salary from $275 per month to $200; ends 12 years of work for this agency.

1918   Joins the American Red Cross. Stationed in France as assistant to Lt. Col. Homer Folks. Assigned to document the effects of the war on the civilian population in the Balkans.

1919   Takes photos of northern France and Belgium; makes this material available to *The Survey*. The photographs are used to inform the public of the conditions of the civilian populace in Europe in a book by Lt. Col. Folks (Homer Folks: *The Human Costs of War*). Returns to New York in June. Works for *The Survey* and *Survey Graphic*, but has difficulty making a living from this work. Moves in a new direction with aesthetic portraits of working people and craftsmen. Changes his advertising to "Lewis Wickes Hine, Interpretive Photography."

1921–29   Works for the NCLC again and for various other agencies such as the Milbank Foundation, the National Consumers League, and the Amalgamated Clothing Workers Union, and also for commercial enterprises. He still has difficulty making a living from photography, despite the fact that his photos are shown at several exhibitions. Plans to sell his house in Hastings-on-Hudson.

1924   Awarded a medal for photography by the Art Directors Club of New York for his portrait *The Engineer*, shown at the Exhibition of Advertising Art.

1930   Takes on a job to document the construction of the Empire State Building, producing more than 100 photos.

1931   Hired by the American Red Cross to document drought conditions in Kentucky and Arkansas rural communities. Works with his son, Corydon, as his assistant. His photographs are exhibited at the Yonkers Art Museum in Yonkers, New York.

1932   Publishes *Men at Work*, a picture book for adolescents, which is chosen as best children's book of the year by the Child Study Association.

1933   Compiles portfolio *Through the Loom* with photos of mill workers. The portfolio is used in *The Survey* and sent to different museums, including the Museum of Modern Art, the Brooklyn Museum, and The Metropolitan Museum, as well as to schools and libraries. Photographs from the *Through the Loom* portfolio are displayed at the 1933 World's Fair. Hine is introduced to Dr. Arthur Morgan of the Tennessee Valley Authority. Hine submits suggestion for a photographic survey, but after some disagreements about the TVA's use of his photographs and because he finds the agency too bureaucratic, he stops working for them

1934–35   Takes on several smaller assignments.

1936–37 Appointed head photographer for the National Research Project of the Work Projects Administration. The project is not completed, but Hine's photos are published in *The Survey* and in David Weintraub and Lewis Hine's *Technological Change*, Philadelphia, 1937.

1938   No income from photographic work or government agencies; strained circumstances. Berenice Abbott and Elizabeth McCausland become interested in his work and urge him to gather his work for a retrospective exhibition for the Riverside Museum in New York. Elizabeth McCausland helps with the selection of photographs and publicity.

1939   Hine, Stryker, and Kellogg arrange sponsorship for the Hine Retrospective exhibition, which opens at the Riverside Museum in January. Exhibition travels to the Des Moines Fine Arts Association Gallery in Iowa and the New York State Museum in Albany. The exhibition is received favorably by the press and leads to several assignments for Hine. Hine's wife passes away.

1940   Sells ten framed enlargements to the New York School of Social Work for $150. Dies after an operation at the Dobbs Ferry Hospital, November 4.

Compiled by Daniela Küster